Quick and easy
CAKES & BAKES

Styling DONNA HAY
Photography QUENTIN BACON

A J.B. Fairfax Press Publication

INTRODUCTION

Baking has never been simpler or more fun than with this selection of quick and easy cakes and bakes. A bowl, a beater and a few minutes in the kitchen is all that it takes to fill the house with the homely warmth and aroma that only a homemade cake or batch of biscuits can provide. There's a recipe on these pages to please everyone and every occasion. So, discover the pleasure of home baking and watch your friends and family return for more . . .

EDITORIAL
Food Editor: Rachel Blackmore
Editors: Kirsten John, Linda Venturoni
Editorial and Production Assistant: Sheridan Packer
Editorial Coordinator: Margaret Kelly
UK Food Consultant: Katie Swallow

Photography: Quentin Bacon
Styling and Food: Donna Hay
Home Economist and Recipe Development: Jody Vassallo

DESIGN AND PRODUCTION
Managers: Sheridan Carter, Anna Maguire
Layout and Design: Lulu Dougherty
Cover Design and Chapter Openers: Michele Withers

Published by J.B. Fairfax Press Pty Limited
80-82 McLachlan Avenue
Rushcutters Bay, NSW 2011, Australia
A.C.N. 003 738 430

Formatted by J.B. Fairfax Press Pty Limited
Printed by Toppan Printing Co., Hong Kong
PRINTED IN HONG KONG

JBFP 346
Includes Index
ISBN 1 86343 184 5

DISTRIBUTION AND SALES
Australia: J.B. Fairfax Press Pty Limited
Ph: (02) 361 6366 Fax: (02) 360 6262
United Kingdom: J.B. Fairfax Press Limited
Ph: (0933) 402330 Fax: (0933) 402234

ABOUT THIS BOOK

INGREDIENTS

Unless otherwise stated the following ingredients are used in this book:

Cream	Double, suitable for whipping
Flour	White flour, plain or standard
Sugar	White sugar

WHAT'S IN A TABLESPOON?

AUSTRALIA
1 tablespoon = 20 mL or 4 teaspoons
NEW ZEALAND
1 tablespoon = 15 mL or 3 teaspoons
UNITED KINGDOM
1 tablespoon = 15 mL or 3 teaspoons
The recipes in this book were tested in Australia where a 20 mL tablespoon is standard. The tablespoon in the New Zealand and the United Kingdom sets of measuring spoons is 15 mL. For recipes using baking powder, gelatine, bicarbonate of soda, small quantities of flour and cornflour, simply add another teaspoon for each tablespoon specified.

CANNED FOODS

Can sizes vary between countries and manufacturers. You may find the quantities in this book are slightly different to what is available. Purchase and use the can size nearest to the suggested size in the recipe.

MICROWAVE IT

Where microwave instructions occur in this book, a microwave oven with a 650 watt output has been used. Wattage on domestic microwave ovens varies between 500 and 700 watts, so it may be necessary to vary cooking times slightly depending on the wattage of your oven.

CONTENTS

Family favourites

*t*his chapter reveals the best of the cake baker's repertoire including the classic Baked Cheesecake, luscious Chocolate Mud Cake and a perfect Strawberry Swiss Roll. For the biscuit tin, who could go past Giant Choc Chip Cookies and the popular Monte Carlo.

CHOCOLATE MUD CAKE

Oven temperature
160°C, 325°F, Gas 3

125 g/4 oz butter
250 g/8 oz dark chocolate, chopped
8 eggs, separated
1 cup/220 g/7 oz caster sugar
1 cup/125 g/4 oz flour, sifted
$^1/_3$ cup/30 g/1 oz cocoa powder, sifted
$^1/_2$ cup/125 mL/4 fl oz cream (double)

CHOCOLATE GLAZE
300 g/9$^1/_2$ oz dark chocolate, chopped
1 cup/250 mL/8 fl oz cream (double)

1   Place butter and chocolate in a heatproof bowl set over a saucepan of simmering water and heat, stirring, until mixture is smooth. Remove bowl from pan and set aside to cool slightly.

2   Place egg yolks and sugar in a bowl and beat until thick and creamy. Sift together flour and cocoa powder. Fold flour mixture, chocolate mixture and cream, into egg mixture.

3   Place egg whites in a clean bowl and beat until stiff peaks form. Fold egg whites into chocolate mixture.

4   Spoon mixture into a lightly greased 23 cm/9 in cake tin and bake for 45 minutes or until cake is cooked when tested with a skewer. Cool cake in tin.

5   To make glaze, place chocolate and cream in a heatproof bowl set over a saucepan of simmering water and heat, stirring constantly, until mixture is smooth. Remove bowl from pan and set aside to cool slightly. Place cake on a wire rack and pour over glaze. Chill.

Chocolate melts faster if broken into small pieces. Make sure your bowl is completely dry before you begin. Leave it uncovered to avoid condensation as just one drop of water will ruin the chocolate. The melting process should occur slowly, as chocolate scorches if overheated.

Makes a 23 cm/9 in round cake

GIANT CHOC CHIP COOKIES

Oven temperature
160°C, 325°F, Gas 3

Here's one for the school lunch box! For something different you might like to use white or milk chocolate or a mixture of dark, milk and white chocolate.

300 g/9$^1/_2$ oz butter, softened
1$^1/_4$ cups/220 g/7 oz brown sugar
$^2/_3$ cup/140 g/4$^1/_2$ oz caster sugar
2 teaspoons vanilla essence
2 eggs, lightly beaten
3$^1/_4$ cups/410 g/13 oz flour, sifted
1 teaspoon baking powder, sifted
375 g/12 oz chocolate chips or dark chocolate, chopped

1   Place butter, brown sugar, caster sugar and vanilla essence in a bowl and beat until light and fluffy. Gradually beat in eggs. Add flour, baking powder and chocolate chips and mix until just combined.

2   Place three tablespoons of mixture in piles well apart onto greased baking trays. Bake for 25 minutes or until golden, cool on wire racks.

Makes 24

EASY ANGEL FOOD CAKE

1 cup/125 g/4 oz flour
1¹/2 cups/330 g/10¹/2 oz caster sugar
10 egg whites
¹/2 teaspoon cream of tartar
1 teaspoon almond essence (optional)

1   Sift flour and half the sugar together and set aside.

2   Place egg whites and cream of tartar in a clean bowl and beat until soft peaks form. Add almond essence, if using. Gradually, beat in remaining sugar and continue beating until thick and glossy.

3   Fold flour and sugar mixture into egg white mixture. Pour into a greased and floured 23 cm/9 in ring tin and bake for 30 minutes or until cooked when tested with a skewer. Cool cake in tin.

Makes a 23 cm/9 in ring cake

Oven temperature
190°C, 375°F, Gas 5

An Angel Cake must be totally fat-free so that it bakes up high with a light, airy texture. Take care when separating the eggs, making sure no yolks mix with the whites and remember to use perfectly clean and dry beaters and bowl.
This cake is delicious served as a dessert with a homemade or purchased chocolate sauce.

Previous pages: Chocolate Mud Cake, Giant Choc Chip Cookies (Teacup *Accoutrement*)
Below: Easy Angel Food Cake

BAKED CHEESECAKE

Oven temperature
160°C, 325°F, Gas 3

For a simple variation, decorate this traditional cheesecake by spreading the top with thick sour cream. Sprinkle with freshly grated nutmeg and garnish with a twist of lemon or lime.

BISCUIT BASE
125 g/4 oz plain sweet biscuits, crushed
30 g/1 oz butter, melted

CREAM CHEESE TOPPING
4 eggs
1 cup/220 g/7 oz caster sugar
440 g/14 oz cream cheese, chopped and softened
155 g/5 oz sour cream
$^1/_2$ cup/125 mL/4 fl oz cream (double)
2 tablespoons lime juice
$^1/_3$ cup/45 g/1$^1/_2$ oz flour, sifted

1 To make base, place biscuit crumbs and melted butter in a bowl and mix to combine. Press mixture over the base of a greased and lined 23 cm/9 in springform tin.

2 To make topping, place eggs and sugar in a bowl and beat until thick and pale. Add cream cheese and beat until smooth. Then beat in sour cream, cream and lime juice. Fold in flour.

3 Pour topping over biscuit base. Bake for 1 hour or until firm. Cool cheesecake in tin.

Makes a 23 cm/9 in round cake

Floral plates and bowl *Accoutrement*

STRAWBERRY SWISS ROLL

Left: Baked Cheesecake
Above: Strawberry Swiss Roll

3 eggs
$^3/_4$ cup/170 g/$5^1/_2$ oz caster sugar
$^3/_4$ cup/90 g/3 oz self-raising flour
1 tablespoon hot water

STRAWBERRY FILLING
4 tablespoons strawberry jam
60 g/2 oz chocolate, grated
1 cup/250 mL/8 fl oz cream (double),
well chilled and whipped
strawberries, to decorate

1   Place eggs and sugar in a heatproof bowl set over a saucepan of simmering water and cook, beating until mixture is thick and creamy. Remove bowl from saucepan and continue beating until cool.

2   Sift flour over egg mixture and fold in with hot water. Pour mixture into a greased and lined 26 x 32 cm/$10^1/_2$ x $12^3/_4$ in Swiss roll tin and bake for 7-10 minutes or until lightly golden.

3   Sprinkle a clean teatowel with a little caster sugar and, working quickly, turn sponge onto teatowel, carefully remove lining paper and trim crusty edges. Carefully roll up sponge in teatowel from short end. Set aside to cool completely.

4   For filling, unroll sponge and spread with jam. Fold chocolate into cream and spread half of this mixture over jam. Reroll sponge and decorate with remaining cream mixture and strawberries.

Serves 8-10

Oven temperature
200°C, 400°F, Gas 6

To make a good sponge, don't rush the process. Whisk the eggs and sugar until thick enough for the beaters to leave a trail across the surface. Be careful not to let the bottom of the bowl touch the water or the mixture will scorch. Keep beating until the mixture is really thick and double in volume before removing the bowl from the saucepan.

THUMB PRINT COOKIES

Oven temperature
190°C, 375°F, Gas 5

185 g/6 oz butter, softened
$^1/_3$ cup/45 g/1$^1/_2$ oz icing sugar, sifted
1 teaspoon vanilla essence
$^1/_2$ cup/60 g/2 oz flour
1 cup/125 g/4 oz self-raising flour
$^1/_2$ cup/60 g/2 oz custard powder
$^1/_4$ cup/60 mL/2 fl oz milk
jam, lemon curd or chopped chocolate

1   Place butter, icing sugar and vanilla essence in a bowl and beat until light and fluffy. Sift together flour, self-raising flour and custard powder. Fold flour mixture and milk, alternately, into butter mixture.

2   Roll tablespoons of mixture into balls and place on greased baking trays. Make a thumb print in the centre of each cookie.

3   Fill thumb print hole with a teaspoon of jam, lemon curd or chocolate. Bake for 12 minutes or until cookies are golden. Transfer to wire racks to cool.

Makes 30

Wrap the dough in plastic food wrap and chill at least 30 minutes to make it easier to shape into balls. For a subtle toasty nut flavour, roll the balls in sesame seeds before making the thumb print and filling.

MONTE CARLO BISCUITS

Oven temperature
190°C, 375°F, Gas 5

125 g/4 oz butter, softened
1 cup/170 g/5$^1/_2$ oz brown sugar
2 teaspoons vanilla essence
1 egg, lightly beaten
1 cup/125 g/4 oz flour, sifted
$^1/_2$ cup/60 g/2 oz self-raising flour, sifted
90 g/3 oz desiccated coconut
$^3/_4$ cup/75 g/2$^1/_2$ oz rolled oats
$^1/_2$ cup/155 g/5 oz raspberry jam

BUTTER CREAM
60 g/2 oz butter, softened
$^1/_2$ cup/75 g/2$^1/_2$ oz icing sugar
1 teaspoon vanilla essence

1   Place butter, brown sugar and vanilla essence in a bowl and beat until light and fluffy. Add egg, flour, self-raising flour, coconut and rolled oats and mix well to combine.

2   Roll tablespoons of mixture into balls, place on greased baking trays and flatten slightly with a fork. Bake for 12 minutes or until biscuits are golden. Transfer to wire racks to cool.

3   To make Butter Cream, place butter, icing sugar and vanilla essence in a bowl and beat until light and fluffy. Spread half the biscuits with raspberry jam and top with Butter Cream. Top with remaining biscuits.

Makes 20

When shaping the biscuits ensure that all are of uniform size and appearance so that each pair is perfectly matched when sandwiched together.

Thumb Print Cookies, Monte Carlo Biscuits

Above: Chocolate Marble Cake
Right: Lemon Syrup Cake

CHOCOLATE MARBLE CAKE

Oven temperature
180°C, 350°F, Gas 4

170 g/5^{1}/$_{2}$ oz butter, softened
^{3}/$_{4}$ cup/170 g/5^{1}/$_{2}$ oz caster sugar
2 eggs, lightly beaten
1^{1}/$_{2}$ cups/185 g/6 oz self-raising flour, sifted
2 tablespoons milk
2 tablespoons cocoa powder, sifted
few drops red food colouring

CHOCOLATE ICING
30 g/1 oz butter, softened
^{1}/$_{4}$ cup/60 mL/2 fl oz milk
1^{1}/$_{2}$ cups/235 g/7^{1}/$_{2}$ oz icing sugar, sifted
^{1}/$_{4}$ cup/30 g/1 oz cocoa powder, sifted

This cake is an attractive idea for children's birthday parties. For something different flavour the pink-coloured portion of the batter with a few drops of strawberry essence.

1   Place butter and caster sugar in a bowl and beat until light and fluffy. Gradually beat in eggs.

2   Fold flour and milk, alternately, into butter mixture. Divide mixture evenly between three bowls.

3   Fold cocoa powder into one portion of mixture. Fold a few drops of red colouring into a second portion of mixture. Leave remaining mixture plain.

4   Drop spoonfuls of the different mixtures into a greased fluted 23 cm/9 in ring tin. Bake for 1 hour or until cooked when tested with a skewer. Stand cake in tin for 10 minutes before turning onto a wire rack to cool.

5   To make icing, place butter, milk, icing sugar and cocoa powder in a bowl and mix until smooth. Spread icing over cold cake.

Makes a 23 cm/9 in ring cake

14

LEMON SYRUP CAKE

125 g/4 oz butter, softened
1 cup/220 g/7 oz caster sugar
2 teaspoons finely grated lemon rind
2 eggs, lightly beaten
1^1/$_2$ cups/185 g/6 oz self-raising flour, sifted
45 g/1^1/$_2$ oz desiccated coconut
1^1/$_4$ cups/315 g/10 oz sour cream
^{1}/$_3$ cup/90 mL/3 fl oz milk

LEMON SYRUP
^{1}/$_3$ cup/90 mL/3 fl oz lemon juice
^{3}/$_4$ cup/185 g/6 oz sugar
^{1}/$_4$ cup/60 mL/2 fl oz water

1 Place butter, caster sugar and lemon rind in a bowl and beat until light and fluffy. Gradually beat in eggs.

2 Stir flour and coconut into butter mixture. Add sour cream and milk and mix until combined. Spoon mixture into a greased 23 cm/9 in fluted ring tin and bake for 1 hour or until cooked when tested with a skewer.

3 To make syrup, place lemon juice, sugar and water in a saucepan and cook over low heat, stirring constantly, until sugar dissolves. Bring to the boil and simmer for 4 minutes or until syrup thickens slightly.

4 Pour half the hot syrup over the hot cake and stand in tin for 4 minutes. Turn cake onto a serving plate and pour over remaining syrup.

Makes a 23 cm/9 in round cake

Oven temperature
180°C, 350°F, Gas 4

Pour or spoon the hot lemon syrup very slowly over the baked cake so that it saturates evenly throughout. For a pretty garnish, simmer long thin strips of lemon peel in a sugar and water syrup until well glazed, drain and arrange over top of cake before they cool.
This cake is delicious served warm as a dessert with thick cream.

One Bowl Butter Cake

Oven temperature
160°C, 325°F, Gas 3

The icing used in this recipe is a basic Butter Icing. By adding different flavourings you can make any flavour you like. To make coffee icing, dissolve 1 tablespoon instant coffee powder in the boiling water. To make lemon icing, replace vanilla essence with 1-2 teaspoons lemon juice. To make orange icing, replace vanilla essence with 1-2 teaspoons orange juice. To make chocolate icing, dissolve 1 tablespoon cocoa powder in the boiling water.

1^1/$_2$ cups/185 g/6 oz self-raising flour
^{1}/$_3$ cup/45 g/1^1/$_2$ oz custard powder
1 cup/220 g/7 oz caster sugar
3 eggs, lightly beaten
^{3}/$_4$ cup/185 mL/6 fl oz milk
1 teaspoon vanilla essence
185 g/6 oz butter, softened

BUTTER ICING
1^1/$_2$ cups/235 g/7^1/$_2$ oz icing sugar, sifted
60 g/2 oz butter
2 tablespoons boiling water
^{1}/$_4$ teaspoon vanilla essence
few drops of food colouring of your choice (optional)

1   Sift flour and custard powder together into a bowl. Add caster sugar and mix to combine.

2   Make a well in the centre of the dry ingredients, add eggs, milk, vanilla essence and butter and beat well for 8 minutes or until mixture is light and smooth.

3   Spoon mixture into a greased 23 cm/9 in round cake tin and bake for 1 hour 20 minutes or until cake is cooked when tested with a skewer. Stand cake in tin for 5 minutes before turning onto a wire rack to cool.

4   To make icing, place icing sugar and butter in a bowl, add boiling water and mix to make an icing of spreadable consistency, adding a little more water if necessary. Beat in vanilla essence and food colouring, if using. Spread icing over top of cold cake.

Makes a 23 cm/9 in round cake

Variations

Orange Butter Cake: Add 2 tablespoons finely grated orange rind to mixture, prepare and cook as above.

Lemon Butter Cake: Add 1^1/$_2$ tablespoons finely grated lemon rind to mixture, prepare and cook as above.

Chocolate Butter Cake: Sift 3 tablespoons cocoa powder with flour and add an additional 1 tablespoon milk to mixture, prepare and cook as above.

Coffee Butter Cake: Dissolve 1 tablespoon instant coffee powder in the milk, prepare and cook as above.

Coffee Butter Cake, Lemon Butter Cake

Chocolate delights

this chapter teams white and dark chocolate with some of its most popular partners — rich cream, mellow liqueurs, roast nuts and luscious fruits — to create eight mouth-watering sensations.

CHOCOLATE CREAM SPONGE

Oven temperature
180°C, 350°F, Gas 4

A light and airy sponge depends on the air incorporated into the eggs during beating. To ensure the air stays where it belongs take care to fold in the flour and remaining ingredients lightly. Do not stir.
To make chocolate curls, have chocolate at room temperature and using a vegetable peeler shave the sides of the chocolate.

4 eggs
1 cup/220 g/7 oz caster sugar
1 cup/125 g/4 oz self-raising flour, sifted
¹/4 cup/30 g/1 oz cocoa powder, sifted
¹/2 cup/125 mL/4 fl oz milk, warmed
15 g/¹/2 oz butter, melted
chocolate curls to decorate

CHOCOLATE CREAM FILLING
1¹/4 cups/315 mL/10 fl oz cream (double)
250 g/8 oz milk chocolate, chopped

1 Place eggs in a bowl and beat until thick and creamy. Gradually beat in sugar.

2 Sift together flour and cocoa powder. Fold flour mixture, milk and butter into egg mixture. Pour mixture into two greased and lined 20 cm/8 in sandwich cake tins and bake for 25 minutes or until cooked when tested with skewer. Turn cakes onto wire racks to cool.

3 To make filling, place cream and chocolate in a heatproof bowl set over a saucepan of simmering water and heat, stirring constantly, until mixture is smooth. Remove bowl from heat and beat until cool.

4 To assemble cake, place one sponge on a serving plate, top with half the filling, then the remaining sponge. Decorate cake with remaining filling and chocolate curls.

Makes a 20 cm/8 in round cake

ESPRESSO LAYERED FUDGE

drinking chocolate, sifted

ESPRESSO LAYER
¹/3 cup/90 mL/3 fl oz very strong black coffee
500 g/1 lb dark chocolate, chopped
410 g/13 oz sweetened condensed milk
90 g/3 oz butter
60 g/2 oz slivered almonds, toasted

WHITE CHOCOLATE LAYER
125 g/4 oz white chocolate, chopped
200 g/6¹/2 oz white marshmallows
¹/4 cup/60 mL/2 fl oz milk

Extending the paper liner an extra few centimetres on two opposite sides of the tin will create handles to help lift the fudge out for easier cutting.

1 To make the Espresso Layer, place coffee, dark chocolate, condensed milk and butter in a saucepan and heat over a low heat, stirring constantly, until mixture is smooth. Cook, stirring constantly, for 3 minutes longer. Stir in almonds and pour mixture into a greased and lined 20 cm/8 in square cake tin. Refrigerate for 2 hours or until firm.

2 To make White Chocolate Layer, place white chocolate, marshmallows and milk in a saucepan and heat over a low heat, stirring constantly, until mixture is smooth. Remove pan from heat and beat until cool.

3 Pour white chocolate mixture over Espresso Layer, dust with drinking chocolate and refrigerate for 2 hours or until firm. Cut into squares.

Makes 40

Previous page: Espresso Layered Fudge, Chocolate Cream Sponge
(Cake stand *Appley Hoare Antiques*)

White Jaffa Cake

WHITE JAFFA CAKE

155 g/5 oz white chocolate, chopped
250 g/8 oz butter, chopped
1 cup/250 g/8 oz sugar
3 eggs, lightly beaten
2 tablespoons grated orange rind
1 tablespoon orange-flavoured liqueur
2¹/₂ cups/315 g/10 oz self-raising flour,
sifted
¹/₄ cup/60 mL/2 fl oz milk
icing sugar, sifted
candied orange peel, to decorate

1   Place white chocolate in a heatproof bowl set over a saucepan of simmering water and heat, stirring, until chocolate melts and is smooth. Remove bowl from pan and set aside to cool slightly.

2   Place butter and sugar in a bowl and beat until light and fluffy. Gradually beat in eggs. Add orange rind, liqueur and cooled chocolate and mix to combine.

3   Add flour and milk to mixture and mix to combine. Pour mixture into a lightly greased 23 cm/9 in fluted ring tin and bake for 30 minutes or until cooked when tested with a skewer.

4   Stand cake in tin for 5 minutes before turning onto a wire rack to cool. Decorate with icing sugar and candied orange peel.

Makes a 23 cm/9 in ring cake

Oven temperature
180°C, 350°F, Gas 4

To prepare candied orange peel, use a vegetable peeler to cut strips of peel from an orange, leaving the bitter pith behind. Cut peel into very thin strips. Blanch for 2 minutes in boiling water and drain. Heat 2 tablespoons sugar and 2 tablespoons water in a saucepan until sugar dissolves, add orange peel and simmer for 8-10 minutes or until all the water evaporates and strips are transparent. Drain. Place on greaseproof paper to dry. Store in an airtight container for up to 2 days.

CHOCOLATE CREAM HEARTS

Oven temperature
180°C, 350°F, Gas 4

125 g/4 oz butter, softened
1 cup/250 g/8 oz sugar
1 teaspoon vanilla essence
1 egg, lightly beaten
2^1/$_2$ cups/315 g/10 oz flour
^{1}/$_4$ cup/30 g/1 oz cocoa powder
1^1/$_2$ teaspoons baking powder
^{1}/$_2$ cup/125 mL/4 fl oz milk
CHOCOLATE CREAM
125 g/4 oz dark chocolate, chopped
100 g/3^1/$_2$ oz butter

1   Place butter, sugar and vanilla essence in a bowl and beat until light and fluffy. Add egg and beat well.

2   Sift together flour, cocoa powder and baking powder over butter mixture and fold in with milk.

3   Knead mixture lightly to form a ball, then wrap in plastic food wrap and refrigerate for 30 minutes. Roll out dough on a lightly floured surface to 3 mm/^{1}/$_8$ in thick.

4   Using a heart-shaped cutter, cut out biscuits, place on greased baking trays and bake for 10 minutes. Transfer biscuits to wire racks to cool.

5   To make Chocolate Cream, place chocolate and butter in a heatproof bowl set over a saucepan of simmering water and heat, stirring constantly, until mixture is smooth. Remove bowl from pan and set aside to cool slightly.

6   Spread half the biscuits with Chocolate Cream and top with remaining biscuits.

Makes 20

Decorate the top of these biscuits by piping crisscross lines of melted dark or white chocolate – or both!

RUM RAISIN NUT BROWNIES

Oven temperature
180°C, 350°F, Gas 4

75 g/2^1/$_2$ oz raisins
^{1}/$_4$ cup/60 mL/2 fl oz brandy
100 g/3^1/$_2$ oz dark chocolate, chopped
125 g/4 oz unsalted butter
2 eggs
^{3}/$_4$ cup/125 g/4 oz brown sugar
1 cup/125 g/4 oz flour, sifted
155 g/5 oz macadamia or brazil nuts, chopped
icing sugar, sifted
drinking chocolate, sifted

1   Place raisins and brandy in a bowl and set aside to soak for 15 minutes or until raisins soften.

2   Place chocolate and butter in a heatproof bowl set over a saucepan of simmering water and heat, stirring constantly, until mixture is smooth. Remove bowl from pan and set aside to cool slightly.

3   Place eggs and brown sugar in a bowl and beat until thick and creamy. Add chocolate mixture, flour, nuts and raisin mixture and mix to combine.

4   Pour mixture into a greased 20 cm/8 in square cake tin and bake for 35 minutes or until firm. Cool brownies in tin. Then cut into squares and dust with icing sugar and drinking chocolate.

Makes 16

For a dinner party dessert top these irresistibly rich and moist brownies with thick cream, a chocolate sauce or berry coulis and a garnish of fresh fruit.

Choc Chip Cashew Cookies (page 24), Peanut Fudge Biscuits (page 24), Chocolate Cream Hearts, Rum Raisin Nut Brownies

PEANUT FUDGE BISCUITS

Oven temperature
180°C, 350°F, Gas 4

60 g/2 oz unsalted butter
125 g/4 oz dark chocolate, chopped
1 cup/220 g/7 oz caster sugar
3 eggs
2 cups/250 g/8 oz flour
1 teaspoon baking powder
1/4 cup/60 g/2 oz sour cream

PEANUT CREAM FILLING
250 g/8 oz cream cheese, softened
1/2 cup/75 g/2 1/2 oz icing sugar
1/4 cup/60 g/2 oz crunchy peanut butter
2 tablespoons orange juice

CHOCOLATE FUDGE
1/2 cup/125 mL/4 fl oz cream (double)
100 g/3 1/2 oz dark chocolate, chopped

These morning or afternoon tea treats are best assembled just before serving, although the biscuit bases can be baked well in advance and stored in an airtight container. Prepare the peanut filling the day before and store, covered in the refrigerator.

1 Place butter and chocolate in a heatproof bowl set over a saucepan of simmering water and heat, stirring constantly, until mixture is smooth. Remove bowl and set aside to cool.

2 Place caster sugar and eggs in a bowl and beat until thick and creamy, then stir in chocolate mixture.

3 Sift flour and baking powder over chocolate mixture and fold in with sour cream. Drop tablespoons of mixture onto greased baking trays and bake for 20 minutes or until biscuits are golden and crisp. Transfer to wire racks to cool.

4 To make filling, place cream cheese, icing sugar, peanut butter and orange juice in a bowl and beat until combined.

5 To make fudge, place cream and chocolate in a heatproof bowl set over a saucepan of simmering water and heat, stirring constantly, until mixture is smooth. Remove bowl from pan and set aside until mixture cools and thickens.

6 To assemble biscuits, spread one biscuit with filling. Make an indent in the middle of the filling with a teaspoon, fill indent with fudge and top with a second biscuit. Repeat with remaining biscuits, filling and fudge.

Makes 12

CHOC CHIP CASHEW COOKIES

Oven temperature
160°C, 325°F, Gas 3

Chocolate 'seizes' if it is overheated or if it comes in contact with water or steam. Seizing results in the chocolate tightening and becoming a thick mass that will not melt. To rescue seized chocolate, stir a little cream or vegetable oil into the chocolate until it becomes smooth again.

155 g/5 oz dark chocolate, chopped
125 g/4 oz butter, softened
1 cup/170 g/5 1/2 oz brown sugar
3/4 cup/200 g/6 1/2 oz peanut butter
1 egg
250 g/8 oz chocolate chips
1 1/2 cups/185 g/6 oz flour, sifted
200 g/6 1/2 oz unsalted cashew nuts,
roasted and chopped

1 Place chocolate in a heatproof bowl set over a saucepan of simmering water and heat, stirring constantly, until smooth. Remove bowl from pan. Set aside to cool.

2 Place butter and sugar in a bowl and beat until light and fluffy. Add peanut butter and egg and beat well. Stir melted chocolate, chocolate chips, flour and cashew nuts into mixture and mix until well combined.

3 Roll two tablespoons of mixture into a ball. Place on a lightly greased baking tray and flatten slightly. Repeat with remaining mixture. Bake for 20 minutes or until cookies are golden. Cool on trays.

Makes 24

CHOCOLATE MOUSSE CAKE

Chocolate Mousse Cake

1 ready-made 23 cm/9 in chocolate
sponge or butter cake
2 tablespoons brandy
chocolate mint sticks or chocolate
caraques for decoration

MOUSSE FILLING
500 g/1 lb dark chocolate, chopped
125 g/4 oz butter
2 egg yolks
1 $^1/_2$ cups/375 mL/12 fl oz cream
(double), whipped

Makes a 23 cm/9 in round cake

1   To make filling, place chocolate and butter in a heatproof bowl set over a saucepan of simmering water and heat, stirring constantly, until mixture is smooth. Remove bowl from pan and set aside to cool slightly.

2   Beat egg yolks into cooled chocolate mixture and fold in cream.

3   Using a serrated edged knife, cut cake into three even layers. Brush each layer with brandy. Place one layer of cake in the base of a 23 cm/9 in lined springform tin. Spoon one-third of the filling over cake in tin. Top with a second layer of cake and half the remaining mousse. Repeat layers. Refrigerate for 4 hours or until firm. Decorate with chocolate mint sticks or chocolate caraques.

The chocolate butter cake recipe on page 16 can be used for this recipe.
Line the springform tin base and sides with baking or greaseproof paper for easier unmoulding. To make chocolate caraques, melt 100 g/3$^1/_2$ oz chocolate in a bowl set over simmering water. Remove from heat and pour a thin layer on to a marble slab or cold baking tray and allow to set until no longer sticky. Holding a large knife with both hands, push the blade away from you across the surface of the chocolate to roll pieces off in long curls.

Garden delights

*e*very family it seems, has a favourite recipe for vegetable cake or fruity loaf. These simple-to-make, everyday bakes are perfect to serve at morning tea and every bit as good as lunch box treats or afternoon snacks.

BANANA NUT UPSIDE-DOWN CAKE

Oven temperature
180°C, 350°F, Gas 4

NUTTY TOPPING
60 g/2 oz butter
$^3/4$ cup/125 g/4 oz brown sugar
3 bananas, sliced lengthwise
100 g/3$^1/2$ oz macadamia or brazil nuts,
roughly chopped

GINGER CAKE
100 g/3$^1/2$ oz butter, softened
$^1/2$ cup/125 g/4 oz sugar
2 eggs, lightly beaten
2 cups/250 g/8 oz flour
1 teaspoon baking powder
1 teaspoon ground ginger
$^1/2$ cup/125 mL/4 fl oz milk

1   To make topping, place butter and brown sugar in a saucepan and cook over a low heat, stirring constantly, until sugar dissolves and mixture thickens to a syrup.

2   Pour mixture over the base of a greased 23 cm/9 in round cake tin. Top with banana slices and nuts and set aside.

3   To make cake, place butter and sugar in a bowl and beat until light and fluffy. Gradually beat in eggs.

4   Sift together flour, baking powder and ginger. Fold flour mixture into butter mixture with milk.

5   Spoon mixture over topping in tin and bake for 50 minutes or until cake is cooked when tested with a skewer. Stand cake in tin for 5 minutes before turning out. Serve hot or warm.

Makes a 23 cm/9 in round cake

Native to Australia, the macadamia nut has a very hard shell and a delicious rich buttery flavour. In most recipes that call for macadamia nuts, brazil nuts can be used instead.

HEARTY FRUIT AND NUT CAKE

Oven temperature
160°C, 325°F, Gas 3

250 g/8 oz butter, softened
1 cup/170 g/5$^1/2$ oz brown sugar
4 eggs, lightly beaten
2 cups/250 g/8 oz flour, sifted
170 g/5$^1/2$ oz sultanas
155 g/5 oz dried apricots, chopped
60 g/2 oz dried pawpaw, chopped
100 g/3$^1/2$ oz unsalted mixed nuts
2 tablespoons finely grated orange rind
$^1/2$ cup/125 mL/4 fl oz apple juice

1   Place butter and sugar in a bowl and beat until light and fluffy. Gradually beat in eggs.

2   Fold flour into butter mixture. Add sultanas, apricots, pawpaw, nuts, orange rind and apple juice and mix to combine.

3   Spoon mixture into a greased 23 cm/9 in fluted ring tin and bake for 2 hours or until cooked when tested with a skewer. Cool cake in tin.

Makes a 23 cm/9 in ring cake

To prevent fruits and nuts from sinking to the bottom of the tin during baking, toss them first in a tablespoon or two of the measured flour listed in the recipe before folding them into the batter. If dried pawpaw is not available simply increase the quantity of dried apricots or use dried pears instead.

Previous page: Banana Nut Upside-Down Cake, Hearty Fruit and Nut Cake

SWEET POTATO AND COCONUT CAKE

250 g/8 oz butter, softened
³/4 cup/185 g/6 oz sugar
2 tablespoons finely grated lime or
lemon rind
2 teaspoons cinnamon
3 eggs, separated
250 g/8 oz mashed sweet potato
45 g/1¹/2 oz desiccated coconut
1 cup/125 g/4 oz flour
1 cup/125 g/4 oz self-raising flour
1 teaspoon bicarbonate of soda
shredded coconut, toasted
candied lime or lemon peel

CREAM AND CITRUS FILLING
250 g/8 oz cream cheese, softened and
chopped
¹/4 cup/45 g/1¹/2 oz icing sugar
2 tablespoons lime or lemon juice

1   Place butter, sugar, lime or lemon rind
and cinnamon in a bowl and beat until
light and fluffy. Gradually beat in egg
yolks.

2   Add sweet potato and coconut and
mix well. Sift together flour, self-raising
flour and bicarbonate of soda. Fold flour
mixture into sweet potato mixture.

3   Place egg whites in a clean bowl and
beat until stiff peaks form. Fold egg whites
into sweet potato mixture.

4   Spoon mixture into two greased and
lined 20 cm/8 in round cake tins and bake
for 30 minutes or until cakes are cooked
when tested with a skewer. Stand cakes in
tins for 5 minutes before turning onto
wire racks to cool.

5   To make filling, place cream cheese,
icing sugar and lime or lemon juice in a
bowl and beat until smooth.

6   To assemble cake, slice each cake in
half horizontally. Place one layer of cake
on a serving plate and spread with one
quarter of the filling. Repeat layers with
remaining cake and filling finishing with a
layer of filling. Decorate with coconut and
candied peel.

Makes a 20 cm/8 in round cake

Oven temperature
160°C, 325°F, Gas 3

Butternut pumpkin is a good
alternative to the sweet
potato in this recipe. Moist
cakes like this are sometimes
difficult to remove from the
baking tin. It's a good idea to
both grease and line the tins
with baking paper.
Candied peel is available
from health food shops and
some supermarkets or you
can make it yourself. See hint
on page 21 for making
candied orange peel.

Sweet Potato and Coconut Cake

Hazelnut Beetroot Cake

Oven temperature
140°C, 275°F, Gas 1

You can bake this mixture in a loaf tin, then slice and store individual servings. To freeze, wrap portions in freezer wrap and seal. To thaw, leave portion in its wrapping and stand at room temperature for about 30 minutes.

250 g/8 oz butter, softened
1 cup/250 g/8 oz sugar
4 eggs, lightly beaten
185 g/6 oz finely grated raw beetroot
200g/6¹/₂ oz hazelnuts, roasted and ground
2¹/₂ cups/315 g/10 oz self-raising flour, sifted
1 tablespoon finely grated orange rind
icing sugar, sifted

1   Place butter and sugar in a bowl and beat until light and fluffy. Gradually beat in eggs.

2   Fold beetroot, hazelnuts, flour and orange rind into butter mixture.

3   Spoon mixture into a greased and lined 20 cm/8 in square cake tin and bake for 1¹/₄ hours or until cake is cooked when tested with a skewer. Stand cake in tin for 5 minutes before turning onto a wire rack to cool. Just prior to serving dust with icing sugar.

Makes a 20 cm/8 in square cake

Cake stand *Appley Hoare Antiques*

WHOLEMEAL MANGO CAKE

Left: Hazelnut Beetroot Cake
Above: Wholemeal Mango Cake

125 g/4 oz butter, softened
1 cup/220 g/7 oz caster sugar
2 eggs, lightly beaten
1 cup/250 mL/8 fl oz mango purée
¹/₃ cup/60 g/2 oz thick yogurt
1 cup/125 g/4 oz self-raising flour, sifted
1 cup/155 g/5 oz wholemeal self-raising
flour, sifted
¹/₂ teaspoon baking powder, sifted

1   Place butter and sugar in a bowl and beat until light and fluffy. Gradually beat in eggs. Beat in mango purée and yogurt.

2   Sift together flour, wholemeal flour and baking powder. Add to mango mixture and and mix to combine.

3   Spoon mixture into a greased and lined 20 cm/8 in round cake tin and bake for 1¹/₄ hours or until cooked when tested with a skewer. Stand in tin for 5 minutes before turning onto a wire rack to cool.

Makes a 20 cm/8 in round cake

Oven temperature
180°C, 350°F, Gas 4

Use either fresh or canned mangoes to make the purée for this cake. If mangos are not available, any thick fruit purée can be used in its place. Try puréed apples in the winter or fresh raspberries in the spring.

31

APRICOT RIPPLE CAKE

Oven temperature
180°C, 350°F, Gas 4

This cake is sure to be a hit as a winter dessert or at a special afternoon tea. Try using pitted dates instead of the apricots, for another fruity variation.

125 g/4 oz dried apricots, chopped
$^1/_2$ cup/125 mL/4 fl oz hot water
125 g/4 oz butter, softened
$^1/_2$ cup/125 g/4 oz sugar
2 eggs, lightly beaten
1$^1/_2$ cups/185 g/6 oz self-raising flour, sifted
1 teaspoon ground cinnamon

1 Place apricots and water in a bowl and set aside to soak for 30 minutes.

2 Place butter and sugar in a bowl and beat until light and fluffy. Gradually beat in eggs.

3 Sift together flour and cinnamon and fold into butter mixture. Spoon half the mixture into a 23 cm/9 in fluted ring tin.

4 Top mixture with apricots and remaining cake mixture. Bake for 45 minutes or until cake is cooked when tested with a skewer. Stand cake in tin for 5 minutes before turning onto a wire rack to cool.

Makes a 23 cm/9 in ring cake

CARAMEL PEAR SLICE

Oven temperature
180°C, 350°F, Gas 4

To cut a slice into even pieces cut it in half lengthwise, then cut each half in half again lengthwise. Then cut the slice in half in the opposite direction and cut each half into thirds. This method of cutting can be varied according to the size and shape you want your pieces to be. For example, for fingers or bars, instead of cutting into thirds at the final stage only cut in half again.

1 cup/125 g/4 oz flour, sifted
$^1/_3$ cup/60 g/2 oz brown sugar
90 g/3 oz butter, melted
440 g/14 oz canned pear halves, drained and sliced

CARAMEL TOPPING
410 g/13 oz sweetened condensed milk
2 tablespoons golden syrup
$^1/_4$ cup/45 g/1$^1/_2$ oz brown sugar
60 g/2 oz butter, melted
90 g/3 oz slivered almonds

1 Place flour, sugar and butter in a bowl and mix to combine. Press mixture into a greased and lined shallow 18 x 28 cm/ 7 x 11 in cake tin and bake for 10 minutes. Arrange pear slices over base.

2 To make topping, place condensed milk, golden syrup, sugar and butter in a bowl and mix to combine. Pour topping over pears and sprinkle with almonds.

3 Bake for 25 minutes or until topping is golden and firm. Cool slice in tin, then cut into bars.

Makes 24

Apricot Ripple Cake, Caramel Pear Slice

STICKY PARSNIP AND PEACH CAKE

Oven temperature
180°C, 350°F, Gas 4

This cake is cooked when it begins to leave the sides of the tin and a skewer inserted into the thickest part comes out clean.
For a dessert or special afternoon tea this cake is delicious served with natural yogurt or lightly whipped cream.

1¹/2 cups/185 g/6 oz self-raising flour
1 teaspoon bicarbonate of soda
185 g/6 oz finely grated raw parsnip
440 g/14 oz canned sliced peaches,
drained and chopped, juice reserved
¹/2 cup/90 g/3 oz brown sugar
¹/2 cup/125 mL/4 fl oz vegetable oil
2 eggs

STICKY PEACH SYRUP
1 cup/250 mL/8 fl oz reserved
peach juice
1 cup/250 g/8 oz sugar
1 tablespoon brandy
¹/2 teaspoon ground ginger

1   Sift together flour and bicarbonate of soda into a bowl. Add parsnip and peaches and mix to combine. Set aside.

2   Place brown sugar, oil and eggs in a bowl and beat until thick and creamy.

3   Fold egg mixture into flour mixture. Spoon mixture into a greased 23 cm/9 in round tin and bake for 45 minutes or until cake is cooked when tested with a skewer.

4   To make syrup, place peach juice, sugar, brandy and ginger in a saucepan and heat over a low heat, stirring constantly, until sugar dissolves. Bring syrup to the boil, then reduce heat and simmer for 5 minutes or until slightly thickened.

5   Turn cake onto a serving platter, slowly pour hot syrup over hot cake. Serve hot or warm.

Makes a 23 cm/9 in round cake

MOIST PASSION FRUIT CAKE

125 g/4 oz butter, softened
1 cup/220 g/7 oz caster sugar
1 tablespoon finely grated orange rind
2 eggs, lightly beaten
2 cups/250 g/8 oz self-raising flour,
sifted
45 g/1^{1}/$_{2}$ oz desiccated coconut
^{3}/4 cup/185 mL/6 fl oz passion fruit pulp

PASSION FRUIT ICING
125 g/4 oz cream cheese, softened
1 cup/155 g/5 oz icing sugar
2 tablespoons passion fruit pulp

Left: Sticky Parsnip and Peach Cake
Below: Moist Passion Fruit Cake

1   Place butter, caster sugar and orange rind in a bowl and beat until light and fluffy. Gradually beat in eggs.

2   Fold flour, coconut and passion fruit pulp into butter mixture. Spoon mixture into a greased and lined 20 cm/8 in round cake tin and bake for 1 hour. Stand cake in tin for 5 minutes before turning onto a wire rack to cool.

3   To make icing, place cream cheese, icing sugar and passion fruit pulp in a bowl and beat until smooth. Spread icing over top of cold cake.

Makes a 20 cm/8 in round cake

Oven temperature
180°C, 350°F, Gas 4

Before turning out a cake, loosen the sides with a spatula or palette knife. Then turn the cake onto a wire rack and immediately invert onto a second wire rack to cool, so that the top of the cake is not marked with indentations from the first rack. If you do not have a second wire rack, invert the cake first onto a clean cloth on your hand then turn it back onto the wire rack.

Plate Accoutrement

Creating muffin magic

*M*uffins are mini-cakes
for busy home bakers.
Freeze them for brunch
treats, quick snacks and
school lunch boxes....or for
when you need to stop and
take a well-earned break.

STICKY DATE MUFFINS

Oven temperature
190°C, 375°F, Gas 5

If 1 cup/250 mL/8 fl oz capacity muffin tins are unavailable, use the standard 1/2 cup/125 mL/4 fl oz capacity tins and bake for approximately half the time recommended. The yield, of course, will be doubled. These muffins make a delicious dessert treat, but are just as good in lunch boxes and for snacks without the sauce.

2 cups/250 g/8 oz self-raising flour
1 teaspoon bicarbonate of soda
1 teaspoon ground cinnamon
1/3 cup/60 g/2 oz brown sugar
90 g/3 oz butter
125 g/4 oz chopped dates
1 egg, lightly beaten
1 cup/250 mL/8 fl oz buttermilk or milk

BRANDY SAUCE
100 g/3 1/2 oz butter
1/4 cup/45 g/1 1/2 oz brown sugar
1 tablespoon golden syrup
1 tablespoon brandy

1 Sift flour, bicarbonate of soda and cinnamon together into a bowl. Set aside.

2 Place sugar, butter and dates in a saucepan and heat over a low heat, stirring constantly, until butter melts. Pour date mixture into dry ingredients, add egg and milk. Mix until just combined.

3 Spoon mixture into six greased 1 cup/ 250 mL/8 fl oz capacity muffin tins and bake for 30 minutes or until muffins are cooked when tested with a skewer.

4 To make sauce, place butter, sugar, golden syrup and brandy in a saucepan and heat over a low heat, stirring constantly, until sugar dissolves. Bring to the boil, then reduce heat and simmer for 3 minutes or until sauce is thick and syrupy. Serve with warm muffins.

Makes 6

APRICOT OAT BRAN MUFFINS

Oven temperature
180°C, 350°F, Gas 4

Serve this muffin for breakfast or brunch fresh and warm from the oven, split and buttered and perhaps with a drizzle of honey.

*Previous page: Sticky Date Muffins, Apricot Oat Bran Muffins
Right: Lemon Poppy Seed Muffins*

2 cups/250 g/8 oz self-raising flour
1 teaspoon baking powder
1 cup/45 g/1 1/2 oz oat bran
60 g/2 oz dried apricots, chopped
60 g/2 oz sultanas
1 egg, lightly beaten
1 1/2 cups/325 mL/12 fl oz buttermilk or milk
1/4 cup/60 mL/2 fl oz golden syrup
90 g/3 oz butter, melted

1 Sift flour and baking powder together into a bowl. Add oat bran, apricots and sultanas, mix to combine and set aside.

2 Combine egg, milk, golden syrup and butter.

3 Add milk mixture to dry ingredients and mix until just combined. Spoon mixture into six greased 1 cup/ 250 mL/8 fl oz capacity muffin tins and bake for 15-20 minutes or until muffins are cooked when tested with a skewer. Serve hot, warm or cold.

Makes 6

LEMON POPPY SEED MUFFINS

2 eggs, lightly beaten
1 cup/250 g/8 oz sour cream
$^1/_2$ cup/125 mL/4 fl oz milk
$^1/_4$ cup/60 mL/2 fl oz oil
$^1/_4$ cup/90 g/3 oz honey
3 tablespoons poppy seeds
1 tablespoon grated lemon rind
2$^1/_4$ cups/280 g/9 oz self-raising flour, sifted

LEMON CREAM CHEESE ICING
60 g/2 oz cream cheese, softened
1 tablespoon lemon juice
$^3/_4$ cup/125 g/4 oz icing sugar

Makes 6

1   Place eggs, sour cream, milk, oil, honey, poppy seeds and lemon rind in a bowl and mix well to combine.

2   Add flour to poppy seed mixture and mix until just combined.

3   Spoon mixture into six greased 1 cup/250 mL/8 fl oz capacity muffin tins and bake for 25-30 minutes or until muffins are cooked when tested with a skewer. Turn onto wire racks to cool.

4   To make icing, place cream cheese, lemon juice and icing sugar in a food processor and process until smooth. Top cold muffins with icing.

Oven temperature
180°C, 350°F, Gas 4

A simple glacé icing is another suitable topping for muffins. To make, sift 1 cup/155 g/5 oz icing sugar into a bowl, slowly stir in 3 teaspoons warm water and a few drops almond or vanilla essence to make a glaze of drizzling consistency. To vary the flavour, omit the essence and substitute the water with 3 teaspoons citrus juice or a favourite liqueur.

Plate Appley Hoare Antiques

CHEESE AND BACON MUFFINS

Oven temperature
180°C, 350°F, Gas 4

4 rashers bacon, chopped
1 egg, lightly beaten
1 cup/250 mL/8 fl oz milk
$^1/_4$ cup/60 mL/2 fl oz vegetable oil
2 tablespoons chopped fresh parsley
2 cups/250 g/8 oz self-raising flour, sifted
90 g/3 oz grated tasty cheese (mature Cheddar)

1   Place bacon in a frying pan and cook over a medium heat, stirring, until crisp. Remove bacon from pan and drain on absorbent kitchen paper.

2   Place egg, milk, oil and parsley in a bowl and mix to combine. Combine flour and cheese. Add flour mixture and bacon to egg mixture and mix until combined.

3   Spoon mixture into twelve greased $^1/_2$ cup/125 mL/4 fl oz capacity muffin tins and bake for 20-25 minutes or until muffins are cooked when tested with a skewer. Serve warm or cold.

Makes 12

An accurate oven is essential for successful baking. It should be well insulated and draught proof, as a discrepancy of a few degrees can ruin baked goods. Regular checking with an oven thermometer helps avoid failures.

POTATO SOUR CREAM MUFFINS

Oven temperature
180°C, 350°F, Gas 4

250 g/8 oz mashed potato
2 eggs, lightly beaten
1 cup/250 mL/8 fl oz milk
$^3/_4$ cup/185 g/6 oz sour cream
60 g/2 oz butter, melted
$2^1/_2$ cups/315 g/10 oz self-raising flour, sifted
3 tablespoons snipped fresh chives

1   Place potato in a bowl. Add eggs, milk, sour cream and butter in a bowl and mix well to combine.

2   Combine flour and chives. Add to potato mixture and mix until just combined. Spoon mixture into six greased 1 cup/250 mL/8 fl oz capacity muffin tins and bake for 25-30 minutes or until muffins are cooked when tested with a skewer. Serve warm or cold.

Makes 6

A properly cooked muffin should have risen well, be slightly domed in the middle (but not peaked!) and be evenly browned. It should also shrink slightly from the sides of the tin.

Potato Sour Cream Muffins,
Cheese and Bacon Muffins

CHOC ROUGH MUFFINS

Muffin tins without a nonstick finish should be greased (and if desired, also lined with paper baking cups) before use. Nonstick tins do not need lining but may need greasing; follow the manufacturer's instructions.

125 g/4 oz butter, softened
$^{1}/_{2}$ cup/125 g/4 oz sugar
2 eggs, lightly beaten
2 cups/250 g/8 oz self-raising flour, sifted
$^{1}/_{4}$ cup/30 g/1 oz cocoa powder, sifted
155 g/5 oz chocolate chips
45 g/1$^{1}/_{2}$ oz shredded coconut
$^{3}/_{4}$ cup/185 mL/6 fl oz buttermilk or milk

1 Place butter and sugar in a bowl and beat until light and fluffy. Gradually beat in eggs.

2 Combine flour and cocoa powder. Add flour mixture, chocolate chips, coconut and milk to butter mixture and mix until just combined.

3 Spoon mixture into six greased 1 cup/ 250 mL/8 fl oz capacity muffin tins and bake for 35 minutes or until muffins are cooked when tested with a skewer.

Makes 6

CLASSIC BLUEBERRY MUFFINS

2¹/₂ cups/315 g/10 oz self-raising flour
1 teaspoon baking powder
¹/₃ cup/90 g/3 oz sugar
2 eggs, lightly beaten
1 cup/250 mL/8 fl oz buttermilk or milk
60 g/2 oz butter, melted
125 g/4 oz blueberries
2 tablespoons coffee sugar crystals

1   Sift flour and baking powder together into a bowl, add sugar and mix to combine.

2   Combine eggs, milk and butter. Add egg mixture and blueberries to dry ingredients and mix until just combined.

3   Spoon mixture into six greased 1 cup/ 250 mL/8 fl oz capacity muffin tins. Sprinkle with coffee sugar crystals and bake for 20-30 minutes or until muffins are cooked when tested with a skewer. Turn onto wire racks to cool.

Oven temperature
200°C, 400°F, Gas 6

Finely shredded orange peel can be added to this mixture to enhance the flavour of the blueberries.
Coffee sugar crystals are coarse golden brown sugar grains. If unavailable, raw (muscovado) or demerara sugar can be used instead.

Left: Choc Rough Muffins
Above: Classic Blueberry Muffins

Makes 6

Lunch box fillers

*f*or healthy snacks and whole-some treats, you need look no further than these fuss-free and easy ideas. These biscuits, scones and slices are great for big-batch baking and all store well — especially inside school lunch boxes!

GLAZED APPLE CAKE

Oven temperature
160°C, 325°F, Gas 3

185 g/6 oz butter, softened
$^1/_2$ cup/100 g/3$^1/_2$ oz caster sugar
3 eggs, lightly beaten
2$^1/_2$ cups/315 g/10 oz flour
2 teaspoons baking powder
$^1/_4$ cup/60 mL/2 fl oz milk
1 teaspoon vanilla essence
3 apples, peeled, cored and sliced

GLAZE
60 g/2 oz butter
$^3/_4$ cup/185 g/6 oz sugar
$^1/_2$ cup/125 mL/4 fl oz milk

1   Place butter and sugar in a bowl and beat until light and fluffy. Gradually beat in eggs.

2   Sift flour and baking powder together over butter mixture, add milk and vanilla essence and fold into butter mixture.

3   Spoon mixture into a greased and lined 23 cm/9 in round cake tin. Arrange apple slices attractively over top of mixture and bake for 1 hour or until cake is cooked when tested with skewer.

4   To make glaze, place butter, sugar and milk in a saucepan and heat over a low heat, stirring constantly, until sugar dissolves. Bring to the boil, then reduce heat and simmer for 15 minutes or until mixture thickens. Pour hot glaze over hot cake in tin. Cool cake in tin.

Makes a 23 cm/9 in round cake

When available, you may want to scatter some fresh blueberries over the apples. A pinch or two of mixed spice can also be added to the glaze if desired.

CHEWY COOKIE BARS

Oven temperature
160°C, 325°F, Gas 3

125 g/4 oz butter, melted
1$^1/_2$ cups/185 g/6 oz sweet biscuit crumbs

CHEWY NUT TOPPING
410 g/13 oz sweetened condensed milk
1$^1/_4$ cups/220 g/7 oz chocolate chips
100 g/3$^1/_2$ oz shredded coconut
155 g/5 oz chopped pecans
1 tablespoon finely grated orange rind

1   Place butter and biscuit crumbs in a bowl and mix to combine. Press into the base of an 18 x 28 cm/7 x 11 in shallow cake tin and set aside.

2   To make topping, place condensed milk, chocolate chips, coconut, pecans and orange rind in a bowl and mix to combine.

3   Pour topping over base and bake for 30 minutes or until golden. Cool in tin, then cut into bars.

Makes 24

The keeping quality of nuts depends on the amount of oil in them. Always check that nuts are fresh before you buy them; check the use-by date and if possible, buy whole shelled nuts and grind them as needed, keeping the remainder in an airtight container in the refrigerator or freezer.

*Previous page: Glazed Apple Cake, Chewy Cookie Bars
Right: Shaggy Dog Lamingtons*

Shaggy Dog Lamingtons

1 x 18 x 28 cm/7 x 11 in butter or
sponge cake
185 g/6 oz shredded coconut
drinking chocolate, sifted

CHOCOLATE CREAM FILLING
$1^1/4$ cups/315 mL/10 fl oz cream (double)
200 g/$6^1/2$ oz dark chocolate, chopped

CHOCOLATE ICING
2 cups/315 g/10 oz icing sugar
2 tablespoons cocoa powder
30 g/1 oz butter, softened
$^1/4$ cup/60 mL/2 fl oz milk

1   Cut cake into 5 cm/2 in squares. Split
each square horizontally and set aside.

2   To make filling, place cream and
chocolate in a heatproof bowl set over a
saucepan of simmering water and heat,
stirring, until chocolate melts and mixture
is smooth. Remove bowl from pan and set
aside to cool. Beat filling until light and
fluffy.

3   Spread filling over bottom half of cake
squares and top with remaining cake
squares.

4   To make icing, sift icing sugar and
cocoa powder together in a bowl, add
butter and mix to combine. Stir in
enough milk to make an icing with a
smooth coating consistency.

5   Dip cake squares in icing to coat
completely. Roll in coconut and dust with
drinking chocolate. Refrigerate until
ready to serve.

Makes 12

To make coating the cake
easier, place coconut and
icing in two shallow dishes or
cake tins. Use tongs or two
forks to dip the cake in the
icing, then place on a wire
rack set over a sheet of
paper and allow to drain for
2-3 minutes before rolling in
the coconut.

EASY BANANA LOAF

Oven temperature
180°C, 350°F, Gas 4

When grating lemon or orange rind, take care not to grate the white pith beneath the skin as it has a bitter unpleasant taste. Grate the rind on a fine-textured grater or use a metal 'zester' tool which consists of a row of tiny holes that cuts and curls fine, long slivers of rind.

250 g/8 oz butter, softened
$^1/_2$ cup/125 g/4 oz sugar
$^1/_2$ cup/90 g/3 oz brown sugar
3 eggs, lightly beaten
1 teaspoon vanilla essence
2 teaspoons finely grated lemon rind
2 cups/250 g/8 oz self-raising flour, sifted
2 ripe bananas, mashed

1   Place butter, sugar, brown sugar, eggs, vanilla essence, lemon rind, flour and banana in a bowl and beat for 5 minutes or until mixture is light and smooth.

2   Pour mixture into a greased and lined 11 x 21 cm/$4^1/_2$ x $8^1/_2$ in loaf tin and bake for 45 minutes or until loaf is cooked when tested with a skewer. Stand loaf in tin for 5 minutes before turning onto a wire rack to cool.

Makes an 11 x 21 cm/ $4^1/_2$ x $8^1/_2$ in loaf

Plate Villeroy & Boch

FRUIT AND CHEESE POCKETS

250 g/8 oz prepared puff pastry

FRUIT AND CHEESE FILLING
170 g/5^1/$_2$ oz sultanas
125 g/4 oz dried apricots, chopped
60 g/2 oz pecans, chopped
^{1}/$_2$ cup/125 g/4 oz ricotta cheese,
drained
1 tablespoon finely grated orange rind
milk
icing sugar

1   To make filling, place sultanas, apricots, pecans, ricotta cheese and orange rind in a bowl and mix to combine.

2   Roll out pastry to 5 mm/^{1}/$_4$ in thick and cut into four 15 cm/6 in squares. Place 2-3 tablespoons of filling in the centre of each pastry square, bring edges together and twist to form a bag.

3   Place on lightly greased baking trays and brush with a little milk. Bake for 15 minutes or until pastry is puffed and golden. Transfer to wire racks to cool. Dust with icing sugar.

Makes 4

Oven temperature
200°C, 400°F, Gas 6

The sweetness of dried fruits should be sufficient for most tastes, however you may like to mix 1-2 teaspoons of honey into the filling.

Left: Easy Banana Loaf
Above: Fruit and Cheese Pockets

Jelly Bean Biscuits

Oven temperature
180°C, 350°F, Gas 4

1^1/4 cups/155 g/5 oz self-raising flour,
sifted
^{1}/3 cup/75 g/2^1/2 oz caster sugar
1 teaspoon vanilla essence
30 g/1 oz desiccated coconut
125 g/4 oz butter, chopped
^{1}/4 cup/60 mL/2 fl oz milk
185 g/6 oz small jelly beans

1   Place flour, sugar, vanilla essence, coconut and butter in a food processor and process until mixture resembles fine breadcrumbs. With machine running, slowly add milk and process to form a soft dough.

2   Stir jelly beans into mixture. Drop tablespoons of mixture onto lightly greased baking trays and bake for 10-15 minutes or until biscuits are lightly browned. Stand on trays for 5 minutes before transferring to wire racks to cool.

Makes 30

Do not store different types of biscuits together as they will absorb flavour and moisture from each other.

Choc Candy Cookies

Oven temperature
160°C, 325°F, Gas 3

125 g/4 oz butter, softened
^{2}/3 cup/100 g/3^1/2 oz brown sugar
^{1}/2 cup/125 g/4 oz sugar
1 teaspoon vanilla essence
1 egg, lightly beaten
1^1/4 cups/155 g/5 oz flour
^{1}/4 cup/30 g/1 oz cocoa powder
1 teaspoon bicarbonate of soda
125 g/4 oz candy-coated chocolates
75 g/2^1/2 oz chopped almonds

1   Place butter, brown sugar, sugar and vanilla essence in a bowl and beat until light and fluffy. Gradually beat in egg.

2   Sift together flour, cocoa powder and bicarbonate of soda. Add flour mixture, candy-coated chocolates and almonds to butter mixture and mix well to combine. Cover with plastic food wrap and refrigerate for 30 minutes or until mixture is firm.

3   Drop tablespoons of mixture onto lightly greased baking trays and bake for 8-10 minutes or until cookies are firm. Stand on trays for 3 minutes before transferring to wire racks to cool.

Makes 30

Be sure to make biscuits a uniform size; not only will they look more attractive but they will also cook more evenly.

Jelly Bean Biscuits, Choc Candy Cookies, Malt Ball Biscuits (page 52)

Malt Ball Biscuits

Oven temperature
180°C, 350°F, Gas 4

90 g/3 oz butter, melted
^{1}/3 cup/60 g/2 oz brown sugar
^{1}/4 cup/90 g/3 oz honey
1 teaspoon vanilla essence
1^1/3 cups/170g/5^1/2 oz flour, sifted
100 g/3^1/2 oz chocolate covered malt
balls, halved

1   Place butter, sugar, honey, vanilla essence and flour in a bowl and mix to combine. Add malt balls and mix to combine.

2   Drop tablespoons of mixture onto lightly greased baking trays and bake for 15 minutes or until biscuits are golden. Stand on trays for 3 minutes before transferring to wire racks to cool completely.

Makes 25

An obvious choice for a child's birthday party, these malty morsels will taste even better teamed with a malted milk shake!

Apricot Oatmeal Slice

Oven temperature
180°C, 350°F, Gas 4

2 cups/315 g/10 oz wholemeal flour
1 teaspoon bicarbonate soda
2^1/2 cups/235g/7^1/2 oz rolled oats
1 cup/170 g/5^1/2 oz brown sugar
200 g/6^1/2 oz butter, melted
icing sugar for dusting

APRICOT FILLING
250 g/8 oz dried apricots
^{2}/3 cup/170 mL/5^1/2 fl oz water
2 tablespoons apricot jam

1   To make filling, place apricots, water and jam in a saucepan and cook over a low heat, stirring, until jam melts. Bring to the boil, then reduce heat and simmer for 5 minutes or until mixture thickens. Remove from heat and set aside to cool.

2   Sift flour and bicarbonate of soda together in a bowl. Return husks to bowl. Add rolled oats, sugar and butter and mix well to combine.

3   Press half the oat mixture over the base of a greased and lined 18 x 28 cm/ 7 x 11 in shallow cake tin. Spread with filling and sprinkle with remaining oat mixture.

4   Bake for 35 minutes or until slice is cooked. Cool in tin, then cut into bars and sprinkle with icing sugar.

Makes 28

This slice is delicious made using any dried fruit. For something different why not try dried dates or figs.

Apricot Oatmeal Slice, Peanut Butter Cookies

PEANUT BUTTER COOKIES

250 g/8 oz butter, softened
1 cup/265 g/8^1/$_2$ oz peanut butter
1 cup/170 g/5^1/$_2$ oz brown sugar
2 eggs, lightly beaten
2^1/$_4$ cups/280 g/9 oz flour, sifted
2 teaspoons bicarbonate of soda, sifted

1   Place butter, peanut butter and sugar in a bowl and beat until light and fluffy. Gradually beat in eggs.

2   Stir flour and bicarbonate of soda together. Add to egg mixture and mix well. Roll tablespoons of mixture into balls, place on lightly greased baking trays and flatten slightly.

3   Bake for 15 minutes or until cookies are golden and crisp. Stand on trays for 3 minutes before transferring to wire racks to cool.

Makes 36

Oven temperature
180°C, 350°F, Gas 4

For a traditional look to these biscuits, flatten the dough balls with a fork so that the tines of the fork leave a chequerboard imprint.

EASY SULTANA LOAF

Oven temperature
160°C, 325°F, Gas 3

Choose sultanas that are
plump and moist-looking;
avoid old fruit that is
shrivelled and hard as it will
not change even during
baking. Sultanas may be
plumped in a little brandy
or dark rum for about
30 minutes before using to
give added flavour to this
simple loaf.

125 g/4 oz butter, softened
$^{1}/_{2}$ cup/90 g/3 oz brown sugar
2 eggs
$^{3}/_{4}$ cup/90 g/3 oz flour, sifted
$^{3}/_{4}$ cup/90 g/3 oz self-raising flour, sifted
$^{1}/_{2}$ teaspoon mixed spice
$^{1}/_{4}$ cup/90 g/3 oz honey
170 g/5$^{1}/_{2}$ oz sultanas

1   Place butter, sugar, eggs, flour, self-
raising flour, mixed spice and honey in a
bowl and beat for 5 minutes or until
mixture is light and smooth.

2   Add sultanas and mix to combine.
Spoon mixture into a greased and lined
11 cm x 21 cm/4$^{1}/_{2}$ x 8$^{1}/_{2}$ in loaf tin.

3   Bake for 1 hour or until loaf is cooked
when tested with a skewer. Stand loaf in
tin for 5 minutes before turning onto a
wire rack to cool.

Makes an 11 x 21 cm/4$^{1}/_{2}$ x 8$^{1}/_{2}$ in loaf

Hazelnut Coconut Slice

1 cup/125 g/4 oz flour
$^1/_4$ cup/60 g/2 oz sugar
100 g/3$^1/_2$ oz butter, softened

NUTTY TOPPING
155 g/5 oz hazelnuts, roughly chopped
45 g/1$^1/_2$ oz desiccated coconut
2 cups/350 g/11 oz brown sugar
$^1/_4$ cup/30 g/1 oz flour
2 eggs, lightly beaten

1 Place flour, sugar and butter in a food processor and process until mixture forms a soft dough.

2 Press dough into the base of a 20 cm/8 in square tin and bake for 10 minutes. Set aside to cool.

3 To make topping, combine hazelnuts, coconut, brown sugar and flour in a bowl. Add eggs and mix to combine.

4 Spread topping over base. Increase oven temperature to 190°C/375°F/Gas 5 and bake for 20 minutes longer or until topping is golden. Cool slice in tin, then cut into squares.

Makes 16

Oven temperature
180°C, 350°F, Gas 4

Fat or shortening in whatever form makes a baked product tender and helps to improve its keeping quality. In most baked goods, top quality margarine and butter are interchangeable.

Left: Easy Sultana Loaf
Above: Hazelnut Coconut Slice

MUESLI NUT BARS

Oven temperature
180°C, 350°F, Gas 4

250 g/8 oz untoasted fruit muesli
100 g/3^1/$_2$ oz sunflower seeds
2 tablespoons sesame seeds
155 g/5 oz dry roasted peanuts
100 g/3^1/$_2$ oz butter
^{1}/$_2$ cup/170 g/5^1/$_2$ oz honey

1 Place muesli, sunflower seeds, sesame seeds and peanuts in a bowl and mix to combine. Set aside.

2 Place butter and honey in a saucepan and heat over a low heat, stirring, until butter melts and mixture is combined. Stir butter mixture into dry ingredients and mix well.

3 Press mixture into a greased and lined 23 cm/9 in square cake tin and bake for 30 minutes or until golden. Cool in tin, then cut into bars.

Watch the baking temperature carefully as the honey in this slice causes it to brown more quickly than if sugar was used.

Makes 24

CHOCOLATE DATE CRUNCH BARS

Oven temperature
180°C, 350°F, Gas 4

1 cup/125 g/4 oz flour
2 tablespoons sugar
60 g/2 oz butter, chopped
2 egg yolks

CHOCOLATE CRUNCH TOPPING
6 egg whites
1 cup/155 g/5 oz icing sugar
250 g/8 oz pitted dates, chopped
250 g/8 oz walnuts, chopped
250 g/8 oz milk chocolate, grated

1 Place flour, sugar and butter in a food processor and process until mixture resembles fine breadcrumbs.

2 With machine running, slowly add egg yolks and process until mixture forms a soft dough. Press dough into the base of a greased and lined 18 x 28 cm/7 x 11 in shallow cake tin and bake for 10 minutes or until golden.

3 To make topping, place egg whites in a bowl and beat until soft peaks form. Gradually add icing sugar, beating well after each addition until mixture is thick and glossy. Combine dates, walnuts and chocolate and fold into egg white mixture. Spoon topping over cooked base.

4 Bake for 40 minutes or until topping is firm to touch. Cool in tin, then cut into bars.

Makes 28

Pecans or hazelnuts are great alternatives for the walnuts in this recipe. You might want to try a mixture of all three nut varieties!

Muesli Nut Bars, Chocolate Date Crunch Bars

Who could resist a slice of savoury bread or damper fresh from the oven. These recipes make the perfect accompaniments for soups and salads. Try filling them with flavoursome fillings for super special sandwiches.

Mexican Cornbread

Oven temperature
180°C, 350°F, Gas 4

Split wedges of this loaf and layer with savoury fillings to create attractive sandwiches. Also delicious served warm and topped with baked ricotta cheese.

2 cups/350 g/11 oz cornmeal (polenta)
2 cups/250 g/8 oz self-raising flour, sifted
125 g/4 oz grated tasty cheese (mature Cheddar)
60 g/2 oz grated Parmesan cheese
12 pitted black olives, sliced
12 sun-dried tomatoes, chopped
100 g/3¹/₂ oz canned sweet corn kernels, drained
3 bottled hot green peppers, chopped finely
2 eggs, lightly beaten
1 cup/250 mL/8 fl oz milk
³/₄ cup/155 g/5 oz yogurt
¹/₄ cup/60 mL/2 fl oz vegetable oil

1 Place cornmeal (polenta), flour, tasty cheese (mature Cheddar), Parmesan cheese, olives, sun-dried tomatoes, sweet corn and green peppers in a bowl and mix to combine.

2 Combine eggs, milk, yogurt and oil. Add egg mixture to dry ingredients and mix until just combined.

3 Pour mixture into a greased 20 cm/8 in springform pan and bake for 1 hour or until bread is cooked when tested with a skewer. Serve warm or cold.

Makes a 20 cm/8 in round loaf

Ham and Mustard Scrolls

Oven temperature
220°C, 425°F, Gas 7

These tangy scone pinwheels make an interesting accompaniment to egg dishes at breakfast or brunch. They can also be reheated briefly in the microwave oven for an afternoon snack.

Previous page: Mexican Cornbread, Ham and Mustard Scrolls

2 cups/250 g/8 oz self-raising flour, sifted
1 teaspoon baking powder, sifted
60 g/2 oz butter, chopped
1 egg, lightly beaten
¹/₂ cup/125 mL/4 fl oz milk

HAM AND MUSTARD FILLING
4 slices smoked ham, chopped
¹/₂ cup/125 g/4 oz ricotta cheese, drained
60 g/2 oz grated tasty cheese (mature Cheddar)
2 tablespoons wholegrain mustard

1 Place flour, baking powder and butter in a food processor and process until mixture resembles coarse breadcrumbs. With machine running, slowly add egg and milk and process to form a soft dough. Turn dough onto a lightly floured surface and press out to make a 1 cm/¹/₂ in thick rectangle.

2 To make filling, place ham, ricotta cheese, tasty cheese (mature Cheddar) and mustard into a bowl and mix to combine. Spread filling over dough and roll up from short side.

3 Using a serrated edged knife, cut roll into 2 cm/³/₄ in thick slices and place on a lightly greased and floured baking tray. Bake for 15-20 minutes or until puffed and golden.

Makes 18

Sesame Pepper Crackers

SESAME PEPPER CRACKERS

1 cup/185 g/6 oz rice flour or
1 cup/125 g/4 oz flour, sifted
2 tablespoons sesame seeds, toasted
1 tablespoon chopped fresh sage or
1 teaspoon dried sage
2 teaspoons pink peppercorns, crushed
125 g/4 oz mascarpone
60 g/2 oz grated tasty cheese (mature
Cheddar)
1 egg, lightly beaten

Makes 30

1 Place rice flour or flour, sesame seeds, sage and peppercorns in a bowl and mix to combine.

2 Combine mascarpone and tasty cheese (mature Cheddar). Add cheese mixture to dry ingredients and mix to form a soft dough.

3 Turn dough onto a lightly floured surface, knead briefly and roll mixture into a sausage shape. Wrap in plastic food wrap and refrigerate for 40 minutes or until firm.

4 Cut into 1 cm/¹/₂ in thick slices, place on lightly greased baking trays and brush with egg. Bake for 10 minutes or until biscuits are golden and crisp. Transfer to wire racks to cool.

Oven temperature
190°C, 375°F, Gas 5

Mascarpone is made from cream. Unsalted and buttery with a fat content of 90 per cent, it is mostly used as a dessert cheese, either alone or as an ingredient. If it is unavailable, mix one part thick sour cream with three parts lightly whipped cream (double), or beat 250 g/8 oz ricotta cheese with 250 mL/ 8 fl oz cream (single) until the mixture is smooth and thick.

BASIL BEER BREAD

Oven temperature
160°C, 325°F, Gas 3

Delicious served spread with olive or sun-dried tomato paste.
Any beer may be used here; you can experiment with light and dark ales and even stout to achieve the different results.

3 cups/375 g/12 oz self-raising flour, sifted
$^1/_4$ cup/60 g/2 oz sugar
6 tablespoons chopped fresh basil
1 teaspoon crushed black peppercorns
$1^1/_2$ cups/375 mL/12 fl oz beer, at room temperature

1 Place flour, sugar, basil, peppercorns and beer in a bowl and mix to make a soft dough.

2 Place dough in a greased and lined 11 x 21 cm/$4^1/_2$ x $8^1/_2$ in loaf tin and bake for 50 minutes or until bread is cooked when tested with a skewer.

3 Stand bread in tin for 5 minutes before turning onto a wire rack to cool. Serve warm or cold.

Makes an 11 x 21 cm/$4^1/_2$ x $8^1/_2$ in loaf

OLIVE SODA BREAD

Oven temperature
200°C, 400°F, Gas 6

The famous Irish soda bread is influenced here by the Mediterranean flavours of fennel and olives. You may use one of the many marinated olives available, if you wish.

125 g/4 oz butter, softened
$^1/_4$ cup/60 g/2 oz sugar
1 egg
3 cups/470 g/15 oz wholemeal self-raising flour
$1^1/_2$ cups/185 g/6 oz flour
$1^1/_2$ teaspoons bicarbonate of soda
$1^1/_2$ cups/375 mL/12 fl oz buttermilk or milk
125 g/4 oz black olives, chopped
2 teaspoons fennel seeds
1 teaspoon coarse sea salt

1 Place butter, sugar and egg in a food processor and process until smooth. Add wholemeal flour, flour, bicarbonate of soda and milk and process to form a soft dough.

2 Turn dough onto a lightly floured surface and knead in olives. Shape dough into a 20 cm/8 in round and place on a lightly greased and floured baking tray. Using a sharp knife, cut a cross in the top. Sprinkle with fennel seeds and salt and bake for 45 minutes or until cooked.

Makes a 20 cm/8 in round loaf

Olive Soda Bread, Basil Beer Bread

BLUE CHEESE AND WALNUT DAMPER

Oven temperature
180°C, 350°F, Gas 4

2¹/₂ cups/315 g/10 oz self-raising flour,
sifted
220 g/7 oz blue cheese, crumbled
1 tablespoon snipped fresh chives
1 teaspoon paprika
155 g/5 oz walnuts, chopped
1 cup/250 mL/8 fl oz buttermilk or milk
1 tablespoon walnut or vegetable oil
60 g/2 oz grated Parmesan cheese

1   Place flour, blue cheese, chives, paprika and 125 g/4 oz walnuts in a bowl and mix to combine.

2   Make a well in the centre of flour mixture, add milk and oil and mix to form a soft dough.

3   Turn dough onto a lightly floured surface and knead until smooth. Roll into a large ball, flatten slightly and place on a lightly greased baking tray. Sprinkle with Parmesan cheese and remaining walnuts and bake for 40 minutes or until damper is cooked.

Makes 1 damper

This loaf tastes wonderful served hot with hearty soups or at room temperature as part of a cheese and fruit board.

CHEESY HERB BREAD

Left: Blue Cheese and Walnut
Damper
Above: Cheesy Herb Bread

2 cups/250 g/8 oz self-raising flour,
sifted
1 teaspoon salt
1 teaspoon chicken stock powder
2 tablespoons chopped fresh rosemary
or 1 teaspoon dried rosemary
2 tablespoons chopped fresh dill
2 tablespoons snipped fresh chives
2 tablespoons chopped fresh sage or
1 teaspoon dried sage
185 g/6 oz grated tasty cheese (mature
Cheddar)
1 egg, lightly beaten
155 mL/5 fl oz milk
30 g/1 oz butter, melted

1 Place flour, salt, stock powder,
rosemary, dill, chives, sage and 125 g/
4 oz cheese in a bowl and mix to combine.

2 Combine egg, milk and butter. Add
egg mixture to dry ingredients and mix to
combine.

3 Spoon mixture into a greased and
lined 11 x 21 cm/4^1/$_2$ in x 8^1/$_2$ in loaf pan,
sprinkle with remaining cheese and bake
for 45 minutes or until cooked when
tested with a skewer. Turn onto a wire
rack to cool.

Makes an 11 x 21 cm/4^1/$_2$ in x 8^1/$_2$ in loaf

Oven temperature
190°C, 375°F, Gas 5

Another time try combining
the flavours of thyme, bay
leaves and fennel seeds with
the rosemary and sage for a
loaf infused with the classic
'herbes de Provence'.

Festive treats

*f*estive holidays or celebrations would be difficult to imagine without a special sweet treat as a centrepiece. This chapter features favourite home baking recipes like Gingerbread Men, Quick Mix Christmas Cake, Easter Cake and Shortbread.

QUICK MIX CHRISTMAS CAKE

Oven temperature
180°C, 350°F, Gas 4

125 g/4 oz butter
1 cup/170 g/5$^{1}/_{2}$ oz brown sugar
1 cup/250 mL/8 fl oz milk
1 kg/2 lb mixed dried fruit
125 g/4 oz unsalted mixed nuts, chopped
$^{1}/_{2}$ cup/125 mL/4 fl oz brandy
1 teaspoon bicarbonate of soda
2 eggs, lightly beaten
1 cup/125 g/4 oz flour, sifted
1 cup/125 g/4 oz self-raising flour, sifted
1 teaspoon ground cinnamon
155 g/5 oz whole blanched almonds

Store this cake in a cool place in an airtight tin or wrap first in cheesecloth, then aluminium foil or plastic food wrap so that it stays moist to the last crumb.

1 Place butter, sugar, milk, mixed fruit, nuts and 2 tablespoons brandy in a large saucepan and heat over low heat, stirring constantly, until sugar dissolves.

2 Bring mixture to the boil, then reduce heat and simmer for 5 minutes. Remove pan from heat and stir in bicarbonate of soda.

3 Transfer mixture to a bowl and set aside to cool slightly. Add eggs, flour, self-raising flour and cinnamon to fruit mixture and mix well to combine.

4 Spoon mixture into a greased and lined 23 cm/9 in square cake tin, decorate with almonds and bake for 1 hour or until cake is cooked when tested with a skewer. Sprinkle remaining brandy over hot cake and cool in tin.

Makes a 23 cm/9 in square cake

CHRISTMAS TREE COOKIES

Oven temperature
180°C, 350°F, Gas 4

185 g/6 oz butter, softened
1 cup/250 g/8 oz sugar
1 teaspoon vanilla essence
1 egg, lightly beaten
2$^{1}/_{2}$ cups/315 g/10 oz flour, sifted
Butter Icing (page 16)
small sweets

If you find the dough sticky or difficult to handle, chill it a little longer or roll it between sheets of nonstick baking paper. Don't add extra flour to the working surface as this will spoil the texture of the biscuits.

1 Place butter, sugar and vanilla essence in a bowl and beat until light and fluffy. Gradually beat in egg.

2 Add flour to egg mixture and mix until just combined. Knead dough into a ball, wrap in plastic food wrap and refrigerate for 45 minutes or until firm.

3 Roll dough out on a lightly floured surface until 3 mm/$^{1}/_{8}$ in thick. Using a Christmas tree cutter, cut out cookies and place on lightly greased baking trays. Bake for 10-12 minutes or until pale golden. Transfer to wire racks to cool completely.

4 Decorate cookies with icing and sweets as shown in picture.

Makes 30

Previous page: Quick Mix Christmas Cake, Christmas Tree Cookies
(Cake stand and plate *The Bay Tree Kitchen Shop*)

SHORTBREAD

200 g/6^1/$_2$ oz butter, softened
^{1}/$_2$ cup/100 g/3^1/$_2$ oz caster sugar
1 teaspoon vanilla essence
2^1/$_4$ cups/280 g/9 oz flour, sifted
^{1}/$_3$ cup/60 g/2 oz rice flour (ground rice), sifted

1   Place butter, sugar and vanilla essence in a bowl and beat until light and fluffy. Add flour and rice flour (ground rice) and mix to combine.

2   Roll out dough on a lightly floured surface to form a 2 cm/^{3}/$_4$ in thick circle.

3   Pinch edges or press dough into a large shortbread mould. Place on a lightly greased baking tray and bake for 25 minutes or until lightly browned.

Makes 1 large shortbread round

Shortbread

Oven temperature
160°C, 325°F, Gas 3

Butter shortbread originated in Scotland as a festive confection particularly for Christmas and Hogmanay.

EASTER CAKE

Oven temperature
180°C, 350°F, Gas 4

185 g/6 oz butter, softened
$^3/_4$ cup/125 g/4 oz brown sugar
2 eggs
$^1/_3$ cup/90 mL/3 fl oz golden syrup
$1^1/_2$ cups/185 g/6 oz self-raising flour,
sifted
$^1/_2$ cup/60 g/2 oz flour, sifted
1 teaspoon ground cinnamon
1 teaspoon ground nutmeg
$^3/_4$ cup/185 mL/6 fl oz milk
foil wrapped chocolate eggs

1 Place butter, sugar, eggs, golden syrup, self-raising flour, flour, cinnamon, nutmeg and milk in a bowl and beat for 5 minutes or until mixture is smooth.

2 Pour mixture into a greased 23 cm/9 in fluted ring tin and bake for 40 minutes or until cake is cooked when tested with a skewer. Stand cake in tin for 5 minutes before turning onto a wire rack to cool.

3 Just prior to serving fill centre of cake with chocolate eggs.

Makes a 23 cm/9 in ring cake

Cool cakes on a wire rack so that the air can circulate freely around them. This prevents cakes getting soggy in the middle and collapsing.

MARSHMALLOW EASTER EGGS

flour, to make moulds
185 g/6 oz dark chocolate, melted

MARSHMALLOW
2 cups/500 g/1 lb sugar
2 tablespoons gelatine
$1^1/_2$ cups/375 mL/12 fl oz water
$^1/_3$ cup/90 mL/3 fl oz liquid glucose
few drops colouring of your choice
few drops of flavouring of your choice

1 Fill two 18 x 28 cm/7 x 11 in shallow cake tins with flour. Using a whole egg, make rows of impressions up to about half the depth of the egg.

2 To make marshmallow, place sugar, gelatine, water and glucose in a saucepan and heat over low heat, stirring constantly, until sugar and gelatine dissolve.

3 Bring to the boil, reduce heat and simmer for 8 minutes. Transfer mixture to a bowl and set aside to cool until warm.

4 Beat marshmallow until thick and white, then colour and flavour as desired. Spoon marshmallow carefully into egg moulds to make half egg shapes. Refrigerate for 2 hours or until set.

5 Remove marshmallow egg halves from flour moulds and brush off excess flour.

6 Sandwich together marshmallows to form egg shapes. Place on a wire rack and drizzle with melted chocolate, allow to set.

Makes 24

Avoid making marshmallow on a hot or humid day. The sugar syrup absorbs moisture from the air as it cools and can make the marshmallow mixture sticky or too soft.

Previous page: Easter Cake, Marshmallow Easter Eggs
(Cake stand *The Bay Tree Kitchen Shop*)

GINGERBREAD MEN

Gingerbread Men

185 g/6 oz butter, softened
³/4 cup/125 g/4 oz brown sugar
¹/4 cup/90 mL/3 fl oz golden syrup
1 egg
2³/4 cups/350 g/11 oz flour, sifted
2 teaspoons ground ginger
1 teaspoon ground cinnamon
¹/2 teaspoon bicarbonate of soda

1 Place butter and sugar in a bowl and beat until light and fluffy. Gradually beat in golden syrup and egg.

2 Sift together flour, ginger, cinnamon and bicarbonate of soda. Add flour mixture to butter mixture and mix to form a soft dough. Divide dough into two portions, wrap in plastic food wrap and refrigerate for 1 hour or until firm.

3 Roll out dough on a lightly floured surface to 5 mm/¹/4 in thick. Using a gingerbread man cutter, cut out cookies and place on lightly greased and floured baking trays. Using a small knife and a drinking straw, make indents to form eyes, mouth and buttons. Bake for 10 minutes or until just golden. Stand on trays for 5 minutes before transferring to wire racks to cool.

Makes 24

Oven temperature
180°C, 350°F, Gas 4

If a gingerbread man cutter is not available, draw the desired shape onto thin cardboard, cut out and use this template as a guide for cutting the outline with the tip of a sharp knife.

73

Simply special

*t*his mouth-watering
collection of best-ever
cakes and gateaux make
impressive dinner party
desserts. Easy-to-prepare,
elegantly presented and
every bit as delicious, these
recipes prove that splashing
out has never been simpler.

CHOCOLATE GLAZED COCONUT CAKE

Oven temperature
180°C, 350°F, Gas 4

250 g/8 oz butter, melted
200 g/6¹/₂ oz desiccated coconut
2¹/₄ cups/280 g/9 oz self-raising flour,
sifted
1¹/₂ cups/330 g/10¹/₂ oz caster sugar
4 eggs
1 cup/250 mL/8 fl oz milk
2 tablespoons dark rum

ORANGE FILLING
2 teaspoons finely grated orange rind
2 teaspoons icing sugar, sifted
³/₄ cup/185 mL/6 fl oz cream (double),
well chilled and whipped

CHOCOLATE GLAZE
375 g/12 oz dark chocolate, chopped
¹/₄ cup/60 mL/2 fl oz vegetable oil
gold dragees

When glazing cakes such as this, place the cake on a wire rack set over a plate or baking tray so that the tray catches any excess glaze as it drips off the sides of the cake.

1   Place butter, coconut, flour, caster sugar, eggs, milk and rum in a bowl and beat for 3 minutes or until well combined. Spoon mixture into a greased and lined 23 cm/9 in square cake tin and bake for 45 minutes or until cake is cooked when tested with a skewer. Stand cake in tin for 5 minutes before turning onto a wire rack to cool. Using a serrated edged knife, split cake horizontally.

2   To make filling, fold orange rind and icing sugar into whipped cream. Spread filling over one layer of cake and top with remaining cake layer.

3   To make glaze, place chocolate in a heatproof bowl set over a saucepan of simmering water and heat, stirring, until chocolate melts and is smooth. Stir in oil and mix to combine.

4   Place cake on a wire rack. Pour glaze over cake, allowing it to run down the sides. Decorate with gold dragees and refrigerate for 1 hour or until glaze is set.

Makes a 23 cm/9 in square cake

BLACK AND WHITE CAKE

Oven temperature
180°C, 350°F, Gas 4

155 g/5 oz butter, melted
2 cups/250 g/8 oz self-raising flour,
sifted
1¹/₂ cups/330 g/10¹/₂ oz caster sugar
²/₃ cup/60 g/2 oz cocoa powder, sifted
2 eggs
1 cup/250 mL/8 fl oz milk
8 dark chocolate truffles
8 white chocolate truffles

WHITE CHOCOLATE ICING
185 g/6 oz white chocolate, chopped
¹/₄ cup/60 mL/2 fl oz cream (double)

For another stylish black and white alternative, drizzle melted dark chocolate over the white chocolate coating after the coating has set.

1   Place butter, flour, sugar, cocoa powder, eggs and milk in a bowl and beat until combined. Spoon mixture into a greased 23 cm/9 in fluted ring tin and bake for 40 minutes or until cooked when tested with a skewer. Allow cake to stand in tin for 10 minutes before turning onto a wire rack to cool completely.

2   To make icing, place chocolate in a heatproof bowl set over a saucepan of simmering water and heat, stirring until melted. Add cream and stir until smooth.

3   Drizzle icing over cake, leaving some of the cake exposed to give a black and white effect. Allow icing to set. Place cake on a serving plate and fill centre with truffles.

Makes a 23 cm/9 in ring cake

ORANGE LIQUEUR LAYER CAKE

6 eggs
1 cup/220 g/7 oz caster sugar
1¹/₂ cups/185 g/6 oz self-raising flour, sifted
¹/₃ cup/90 mL/3 fl oz warm milk
candied orange peel, to decorate

ORANGE FILLING
2 cups/500 mL/16 fl oz cream (double)
¹/₄ cup/60 mL/2 fl oz orange-flavoured liqueur
2 tablespoons icing sugar
2 teaspoons finely grated orange rind

1   Place eggs in a bowl and beat until thick and creamy. Gradually add sugar, beating well after each addition until mixture is creamy.

2   Fold flour and milk into egg mixture. Pour mixture into two greased and lined 26 x 32 cm/10¹/₂ x 12³/₄ in Swiss roll tins and bake for 10-12 minutes or until cake is cooked. Stand cakes in tins for 5 minutes before turning onto wire racks to cool. Cut each cake into three equal pieces.

3   To make filling, place cream, liqueur, icing sugar and orange rind in a bowl and beat until thick.

4   To assemble, place a layer of cake on a serving plate and spread with filling. Repeat layers, finishing with a layer of filling. Spread remaining filling over sides of cake and decorate with candied orange peel.

Serves 6-8

Oven temperature
180°C, 350°F, Gas 4

A successful whisked sponge depends on a thick and creamy egg and sugar mixture. This takes 8-10 minutes using an electric mixer and leaves a thick ribbon trail when the beaters are lifted from the mixture.
To make candied orange peel see hint on page 21.

Previous page: Chocolate Glazed Coconut Cake, Black and White Cake (Cake stand *The Bay Tree Kitchen Shop*)
Below: Orange Liqueur Layer Cake

Plate *The Bay Tree Kitchen Shop*

CARAMEL HAZELNUT CAKE

Oven temperature
180°C, 350°F, Gas 4

Caramelised hazelnuts make an elegant garnish for this European-style dessert cake. To make, gently melt a little granulated sugar in a frying pan until it turns a pale golden colour. Remove from heat, quickly drop in whole toasted hazelnuts and stir briskly with a wooden spoon until well coated. Cool on an oiled baking sheet or on baking paper.

4 eggs
1 cup/220 g/7 oz caster sugar
1¹/4 cups/155 g/5 oz self-raising flour, sifted
¹/3 cup/45 g/1¹/2 oz ground hazelnuts
¹/2 cup/125 mL/4 fl oz milk, warmed
15 g/¹/2 oz butter, melted
60 g/2 oz whole hazelnuts

CARAMEL AND CREAM FILLING
2 cups/500 mL/16 fl oz cream (double)
1 tablespoon icing sugar, sifted
375 g/12 oz soft caramels

1 Place eggs in a bowl and beat until thick and creamy. Gradually add caster sugar, beating well after each addition, until mixture is creamy.

2 Combine flour and ground hazelnuts. Fold flour mixture, milk and butter into egg mixture. Pour mixture into two greased and lined 20 cm/8 in round cake tins and bake for 25 minutes or until cakes are cooked when tested with a skewer. Turn onto wire racks to cool.

3 To make filling, place cream and icing sugar in a bowl and beat until thick. Place caramels in a saucepan and cook, stirring, over a low heat until caramels melt and mixture is smooth. Remove from heat and set aside to cool slightly.

4 To assemble, split each cake in half horizontally using a serrated edged knife. Place one layer of cake on a serving plate, spread with cream mixture, drizzle with caramel and top with a second layer of sponge. Repeat layers, finishing with a layer of filling and drizzling with caramel. Decorate top of cake with whole hazelnuts.

Makes a 20 cm/8 in round cake

Caramel Hazelnut Cake

Fig and Mascarpone Cake

FIG AND MASCARPONE CAKE

32 sponge fingers
$^1/_2$ cup/125 mL/4 fl oz marsala or sweet sherry
6 fresh figs, sliced
extra figs to decorate

MASCARPONE CUSTARD
3 tablespoons custard powder
2 tablespoons caster sugar
1 cup/250 mL/8 fl oz milk
1 cup/250 mL/8 fl oz cream (double)
1 teaspoon vanilla essence
375 g/12 oz mascarpone

1 To make custard, place custard powder, sugar, milk, cream and vanilla essence in a saucepan and whisk until mixture is smooth. Cook over a low heat, stirring constantly, until custard thickens. Remove pan from heat and set aside to cool. Fold mascarpone into cooled custard and set aside.

2 Line a 23 cm/9 in springform tin with nonstick baking paper and line the base with half the sponge fingers. Sprinkle with half the marsala, top with half the sliced figs and half the custard. Repeat layers to use all ingredients. Cover with plastic food wrap and refrigerate for 4 hours or until cake has set.

3 Remove cake from tin. Decorate the top with extra figs.

Makes a 23 cm/9 in round cake

When figs are not in season, fresh strawberries make a suitable substitute for this elegant charlotte.

79

FLAKY PASSION FRUIT GATEAU

Oven temperature
200°C, 400°F, Gas 6

The final assembly of this gâteau should be done just prior to serving so that the pastry does not go soggy. However the filling can be prepared up to a day in advance and stored, covered in the refrigerator until required. The pastry rounds can be cooked up to a week in advance and stored in an airtight container.
Use a fluted pastry wheel when cutting out the pastry rounds to create a decorative edge to this gâteau.

Flaky Passion Fruit Gâteau

440 g/14 oz prepared puff pastry
milk
2 tablespoons sugar
2 cups/500 mL/16 fl oz cream (double),
well chilled and whipped
2 tablespoons passion fruit pulp
1 tablespoon thin lime rind strips

PASSION FRUIT FILLING
$^1/_2$ cup/125 mL/4 fl oz passion fruit pulp
2 tablespoons lime juice
60 g/2 oz butter
2 eggs
$^1/_3$ cup/75 g/2 $^1/_2$ oz caster sugar

1 To make filling, place passion fruit pulp, lime juice, butter, eggs and caster sugar in a heatproof bowl set over a saucepan of simmering water and cook, stirring constantly, until mixture thickens. Remove bowl from pan and set aside to cool.

2 On a lightly floured board, roll out pastry to 3 mm/$^1/_8$ in thick and cut out three 20 cm/8 in rounds. Place on lightly greased baking trays, brush with a little milk and sprinkle with sugar. Bake for 12 minutes or until pastry is puffed and golden. Tranfer to wire racks to cool.

3 To assemble gâteau, split pastry rounds in half horizontally. Place one pastry layer on a serving plate, spread with some of the cream and drizzle with some of the filling. Repeat layers, finishing with a layer of cream.

4 Decorate top of gâteau with passion fruit pulp and lime rind strips. Serve immediately.

Makes a 20 cm/8 in round cake

Cake stand *The Bay Tree Kitchen Shop*

INDEX

ACKNOWLEDGEMENTS

Accoutrement Cookshops
611 Military Road
Mosman, Sydney
Ph: (02) 969 1031
Carousel Shopping Centre,
Bondi Junction, Sydney
Ph: (02) 387 8468

Appley Hoare Antiques
55 Queen Street,
Woollahra, Sydney
Ph: (02) 362 3045

Bay Tree Kitchen Shop
40 Holdsworth Street,
Woollahra, Sydney
Ph: (02) 328 1101

Villeroy & Boch
Available from major department
stores and gift suppliers
Ph: (02) 975 3099 enquiries